MADCAP

poems by

James Henry Zukin

Finishing Line Press
Georgetown, Kentucky

MADCAP

MASTERS OF
DISASTER CAPITALISM

AND

HORRORS OF WAR

ACKNOWLEDGMENTS

I have been profoundly influenced by the guiding light of Christopher Merrill
at the week long Todos Santos Writers Workshop for the last five years. He
directs the International Writing Program at the University of Iowa. His many
books of poetry and prose have been translated into nearly forty languages.

Laurel Ann Bogen, formerly of the Board of Beyond Baroque and a legendary
poet in her own right, has led over 200 weekly workshops I have attended
and countless sessions showing me the path to poethood and the mobility of
verse.

Publisher: Leah Huete de Maines
Editor: Christen Kincaid
Author Photo: Maggie Smith Taplin
Cover Design: Elizabeth Maines McCleavy

Order online: www.finishinglinepress.com
also available on amazon.com

Author inquiries and mail orders:
Finishing Line Press
PO Box 1626
Georgetown, Kentucky 40324
USA

Contents

INTRODUCTION

I spend my days arranging mergers, writing poetry and enjoying life. A poet banker is a life of contradictions and contretemps. At school and in life I have two sets of clothing and an identity that lives in neither. I am most proud of parenting five children and most humbled by a loving wife who forgives me before I earn it.

James Henry Zukin

MASTERS OF
DISASTER CAPITALISM

Tiananmen Square 30 Years On

I share my pu-er tea with Sweeper Ho
the best souvenir salesman in all of China

we Chinese are a family that suffered a great tragedy
our students exist in a warp of crying time
they avoid mirrors to not see for themselves
the unspeakable torment that surrounds them

each morning I stop by his kiosk
to share a cup of tea and read The People's Daily
we speak in code with our friend Fu Weici
who goes on and on about Tiananmen Square

the blind child is unable to save China the magic words to
free our people are trapped inside the child's mind with no
laboratory to experiment with freedom

almost finish my tea
but when Sweeper Ho joins in

the backward facing gang of four cowards
brought mayhem to an impoverished land
a little red book inspires a revolution

Fu Weici continues in his despondent voice

Mao's minions take to the floor
for the last dance of the People's Polka
the communist man lives on as a statue
while anarchy that crazed fat rooster
wreaks havoc in the hen house

I share a poem written 30 years ago

how plentiful are the red
watermelons this year
how carefully the people
on the crowded streets eat
the sweet fruit then spit seeds
like bullets into the gutter
never to drip juice
on the blood of the students

The Viper Club

I preen like an Imperial Dragon
jaw thrust out ready to take on all comers.
A captain of industry standing on the Shanghai Bund
wearing a Daddy Warbucks cashmere coat.

I wait for my new friend Chairman Ja.
We met at a Paris Club meeting
eating pâté at a stand up luncheon
discussing the intrigues of the members

who control the funding of the poor countries
being force fed dollars they could never never repay.
"How dare they borrow so much?" ask the members
representing vestigial institutions of colonial power.

Chairman Ja arrives in a Chinese SUV
dressed in a Mao jacket.
He takes me to a three story restaurant
with a neon facade of flashing snakes.

We enter the Viper Lounge where
pools of piranhas and puffer fish greet us.
Over dinner we craft a plan to stretch out
the dubious debts of insolvent countries.

Ja orders the house specialty of baby vipers in hot oil.
Soon a steaming pot is brought to the table.
I look in to see vipers furiously splash and flash
rows of pointed white teeth evoking the Joker's smile.

"Eat from the tail end" warns the waiter.
I pick up the tongs ready to bite into a viper.
It spins around and sinks razor sharp teeth
deep into my plump pink cheek.

Chairman Ja looks at my bloody face and laughs
takes out a rank hanky and uses it to dab my wound.
He recovers his composure looks me in the eye and says
"We are blood brothers, Chinese style, you bleed I smile."

I have been initiated into the Viper Club.

Madame Chou's Revenge

I extend my hand and say
"may a thousand ventures bloom"
Madame Chou is famous for getting
foreign devils to eat horrid things
she is gleefully telling the story
of her great humiliation of a banker

D. Donald D. has a Choate-Yale pedigree
now 40 and a Senior Managing Director
at an eponymous Wall Street bank
"Call me Don" he says while snapping
custom made yellow suspenders

he had insulted Madame Chou
at a signing ceremony a year ago
held to celebrate this deal closing now
by saying, "leave the final terms to me"
Madame Chou's father was on
the Great March with Mao she was
called the Dragon Lady for good reason

when she turned to Don and said
"The Chef has a special delicacy
flown in from Mongolia just for you!"
the table twittered and Don licked his lips

with great fanfare a retinue
in white togas emerged from the kitchen
a large China tureen was presented
the aspic puree with dong is ladled into Don's bowl
he slurps it up and pats his lips
declared it to be the best dish he has ever tasted

he asks if the sausage was a bratwurst
Madame Chou smiles and says it is poached horse dong

Zahir and Zhou

His Excellency Minister Zahir exhausted
from arduous Baghdad/ Paris/ Beijing flight
Chinese demand midnight banquet
cold dishes sit half eaten in wilted flower beds
cavalier State Minister Zhou arrives late
Minister Zahir takes few bites lists left
falls asleep sitting upright propped up

Iraq pauses talks play a game of slight for slight
call for early dinner at notorious Scheherazade
garish Beijing spot sporting bevy of belly dancers
Zidane draped in 7 veils swoops off the stage
slaps the back of Zhou's head with a mysterious
twist…Zahir leans over me to whisper "tit for tat"

The talks have ground down and halt
China demands promised oil to no avail
Iraq demands debt swap for oil or no deal

Zahir studies mantle adorning break out room
pulls clock from wall exposes microphones
I ask my client "Minister Zahir, can I tell Zhou you
will supply power to China's wells in Iraq?
am told so big is his desk he can't reach agreement
in waltzes Zhou without a care in the world
invites Zahir to take a walk around the grounds
standing 6 foot 4 to 4 foot 6 quite the pair of loafers

shoes echo hardwood floor groans in response
Beijing Imperial Palace guest house trembles
His Excellency Minister Zahir stands tall
State Minister Zhou stoops down
walk together translators dismissed
share bawdy big desk jokes in broken English

arm in arm bonded ministers return to say
millions of oil barrels once delayed will flow
across oceans leaving billions of dollars unpaid
Zahir triumphant returns home to acclaim
Zhou's fate decreed sent alone to the Steppes

Liberia's Last Dollar

We are sitting on stools made of elephant forelegs
sorting through records marbled with green mold
in the damp basement of the Liberian Finance Ministry.
Some call us stock shredders grift grinders reminders
of debt stretching time buyers for countries dialing for dollars.

Others applaud our taking borrowed money addicts
through withdrawal on drip fed dollars from dealers
of last resort who distort loan balances and humiliate
stretched sovereigns who step into the vacuum
left by bribe imbibed former ministers as
US forgives loans just as China makes new ones.

Looking for old lenders we place ads and send letters
slip notices under annual meeting hotel room doors.
"If Liberia owes you money please join us May 3rd
at the IMF in meeting Room D". Soon it fills with suits
and dashikis waiting to take Liberia's last dollar.
We take the point with briefing books that boldly outline
the offer of 3c on the dollar and say take the cash now.
Holdouts will be last in line lucky to be paid out in 10 years.

When the most distinguished spokesman for France
in a cashmere suit and silk Hermès scarf rises up
the room falls silent. In his venomous voice he asks
"this is a sham offer why not just write off the debts?"
I say "have you visited Liberia lately,
seen the stunted and wasting children?"

"This is all Liberia can pay."

Gold Shipwreck Rum

Jacob Zuma and I sit at his son Innocent's graduation
he gives a contemptuous Commencement Address
a grand vision for South Africa's bright future
told by a Zulu king with absurd economic predictions
shares his predilection for wine into water fantasies
with stories of his sexual prowess and magnificent member

I talk to him about loan sharks living in African tenements
invisible native imposters with money to burn
in the dead of night ready to make usurious loans
they bring in "contract" labor to mine the earth's riches
and fund warlord's secret Swiss bank accounts

Zuma describes his rape trial testimony to me in detail
he sat with his god-daughter at the home of her father
she flapped her knees apart and together he said
this was an invitation so he "gave her what she wanted
picked her up and threw her to the ground"

in response the South African jury hangs justice itself
their verdict of innocent returns him in triumph to his homeland
where villagers who fear and idolize him turn out in droves
loyal sons he names Innocent who never was
and Goodwill who has none celebrate with Perfectum
the Witch Doctor who serves them Gold Shipwreck Rum.

here I am sitting with these monsters watching
Zuma use his glib tongue the Prince of Plunder hums
"Call me the Duke of Darkness pile the bribes high
watch me outwit the witless and foil the feeble minded"
he declares his victory in the Presidential election
calls it the natural selection of his party for eternity

Zuma ends up in jail as an inverted Nelson Mandela

The Cannibal President

Uncle John calls with bad news
his Kenya Truck Company is in crisis
the Uganda factory blown to smithereens
by a mysterious group of Scottish mercenaries

the spare parts for Idi Amin's army
vaporized in the depot that held them
Amin's threatened invasion of Tanzania
now without spare parts or tires
is stopped dead in its tracks

I am most distressed to hear this
my frame of reference is a personal one
a long planned summer internship
in Kenya with friends has gone up in smoke

imperious in manner and impervious to advice
Amin shreds Uganda's social fabric
a monster adept at using guile who hides
hunger for violence behind a winning smile
this punch drunk most cunning liar
charming face slapper, notorious back stabber
tortures mutilates and decimates his people

feared squads of killers throw cripples to the Nile alligators
thousands of protesting soldiers killed in their barracks
he plots his one time ally now rival's aborted assassination
brutally attacks Israeli "friends" who refuse to sell him arms

after his coup euphoric supporters dance in the street
celebrating the liberation of Uganda from its imperialist past
he proclaims himself "The Lord of all Beasts of the Earth"
brags that he is a cannibal "I have eaten human meat"
he says on many occasions "it is saltier than leopard meat"

The Harlot

MadCap is an informal group of sovereign debt negotiators.
IMF officials and bankers. We gather together
in the lounge of the Harlot DC restaurant
after the IMF/World Bank annual meetings. As we say
"What we share at the Harlot, stays with the Harlot."
We take turns sharing our favorite stories with friends.

A minor emirate is about to default. The Gulf Post
has a story about its twin emirs. They issued Fatwa
decrees the other must die. They have arrived as delegates
to the debt negotiations I facilitate. Alarmed, I ask them
to withdraw their Fatwas so we can get down to business
They jump up, call each other "Brother" and embrace.

In 1955 after Argentina defaulted again on its debts,
the lender countries created the Paris Club to negotiate
as one. Spencer Allatt mentions this in a meeting with officials
from Ecuador and Argentina, who argue over which of them
has defaulted the most often? Spencer totals up the numbers
and Ecuador wins 6/5. He wonders who would make these loans?

My Uncle John sells GM trucks in Africa on a recent trip he buys
a large diamond and hides it in the head of his walking stick.
At US Customs they find the diamond and levy a significant duty
Uncle John convinces the Customs officer to call my Aunt Jo
to ask her to pick him up and pay the duty. When the agent calls
she pauses and says, "ask him who did he buy the diamond for?"

Leaving the Asia Development Bank meeting, we drive by rioters
holding "Stop the IMF" posters. They have turned a police car
on its side. This is a dicey situation. Carlos Espinoza is wearing
a Manila Lions t-shirt and shorts and the rest of our team is in suits.
One asks what will we do if they demand we get out of the car?
Carlos jokes "what will you do Señor, I am the driver's cousin."

Sappuku

Peter Yamagata and I are in a 17th century
Kyoto tea house that was dismantled and rebuilt
inside the penthouse of a sleek Tokyo skyscraper.
We are seated on zabuton at a traditional chabudai table
Chairman Takeda is hosting us to an 8 course banquet
we are here to celebrate the sale of his family's business.

A cedarwood bento box is given to each guest
containing a house specialty of fermented rice balls
served in fine Noritaki china of exquisite delicacy.
Veiled insults are being traded while Namazake
Sake is being poured into small jade cups.

Seated behind each guest is their personal geisha
for the evening Fumiko-san is here to serve my every need
her name means "child of treasured beauty."
She is wearing a blue silk kimono embedded with scenes
of intricately woven tea houses around a serene lake.

The spell she has begun to cast over me is broken
when Takeda-san hands me a small black velvet box.
"Zuki-san" he says, "allow me to present you with a gift"
I open it with trepidation to find an ornate hand carved
ivory objet d'arte shaped like a small buffalo horn.

The Yamagata clan were honored hereditary vassals
of the Tokugawa Shogunate that once ruled Japan
enemies of Takeda-san's ancestors, the Toyama Daimyos.
Their rivalry exists to this day and at this banquet!
When Peter saw what was in the box he jumps up

runs from the table screaming a high pitched ayieee.
I run after him and try to calm him down to no avail.
He gives me a distraught look and through tears says
"Because of me you have lost face I must commit
Sappuku." I told him to not disembowel himself.

I seek out Fumiko-san and ask what just happened?
She tells me that Takeda-san has insulted me because his
and Peter's ancestors are enemies for 250 years.
"The gift he gave you" she says "is called a Zuki."
it is a woman's self pleasuring device.

Department of Wet Affairs

Sergei is on a mission to kill a charismatic
Russian, the indomitable Alexander Litvinenko.
A legendary spy in the KGB, Sergei was trained
at the "Coca Cola City" campus in their Urals

where KGB spies learn American English.
They drive Ford trucks and live in tract homes
at the Dzerzhinsky Higher School for Spies
with a specialization in various deadly poisons.

He dons the waiter's garb his scarred
hands now gloved pushes the tea trolley
on the stain covered rug to Litvinenko's
hotel room. Pours the Polonium 210

into a cup of chamomile tea,
knocks on the door, limps in
"pour the tea?" he asks, then leaves.
Alexander, ex-KGB takes a few sips

goes outside to hail a black cab
to Pall Mall. He enters the lobby
is whisked up to the 5th floor.
Feeling funny looking pasty

leaves quickly staggers and falls
in a faint. An ambulance is called
takes him to Battersea Hospital where
he coughs up blood and dies in the ER.

Sergei returns to Dzerzhinsky a hero.

Spying for Dad 1968

I am visiting my family in Athens over the summer.
I find 3 passports when searching for cuff links in my
father's study. They have his picture with different names
and countries. One is a US diplomatic passport.

When I casually drop the passports on his desk he smiles
and says the time has come for me to work with him.
He tells me how he turns his Russian ham radio
friends into contacts that can be useful for the DIA.

Dad's friend Joe Martin calls me to arrange a time to meet.
I am getting my first briefing, heady stuff for a 19 year
old UC Berkeley undergraduate. As Joe explains my mission
the Everbrite Foundation gave the Doha Hospital

a small medical center shipped in large containers. When they
arrived the dock workers loaded the cargo into trucks but were
not paid the customary gratuity, so the last truck was hijacked.
My mission is to make visual contact and pass Joe the gratuity.

I spot Joe Martin dressed in an embroidered ottoman vest
then find my way to the central harem in the Casbah.
When a smoke bomb goes off in a planned diversion
I slip him the wallet and disappear in a myriad of tents.

I return to the Hilton to pack my bags and fly home
Dad picks me up at the gate and shakes my hand.
It is the only time I can recall him shaking my hand
it felt creepy and the whole experience left me cold.
We return home and I tell dad I was done being a spook.

HORRORS
OF
WAR

Dispatches from Baghdad

Drop and Cover Bar is always open
officers down drinks with war widows
in burkas of gelignite guncotton
look killing eyes flash from within
telegraph torment yet to begin

the rest is theatre

war dogs call the Green Zone home
provide pallets of soiled greenbacks
fund the grave diggers flea market
for corpse bags second-hand caskets
undersize crutches and flak jackets

everything changes

sand princes wed nitroglycerin brides
ceremonies end in limb fireworks
any man a weapon any woman
a prisoner any child a martyr
every day dream for sale or barter

the unknown soldier

Exhausted Iraqi soldiers dig in
wonder who they are dying for
soon return to corrugated tin hovels
fill old closets with single sleeve
blood splatter British fatigues

is the first to die

The Art of Buying Bullets

the Bell helicopter sets down in a gorge
behind a sand dune outside Baghdad
I push the Glock toggle off safety
grab my battered backpack and set out
to find the camouflaged MRAP

a Heckler & Koch machine gun sits in a bed
strewn with a great jumble of ammo belts
Zuhair the gunner spits out a plug of chew
asks "pay as we go or flat fee for bullets?"
used if under fire on the road

I reach into my Doc Martens combat boot
pull out a sealed pack of a hundred hundreds
tell him there is a bonus for not firing a shot
MRAP rumbles forward like an aged rhino
with pockmarks covered by shrapnel

we arrive at the Kristal Hotel in darkness
I find working lights and running water
go up to the 8th floor and flick on the lights
unaware a terrorist named Abu Nabil
sits outside on his haunches smoking nettles

he removes the cover on his rocket cart
sees my light go on and tightens the launcher,
aims the MPAD at my room and fires
a huge roar then the room next to me is gone
its door flies through the wall across the hall

SatNav in hand I hit the floor
call my wife at home
"Honey no worries I'm going to sleep.
Ignore the evening news. Just propaganda."

Dinner with Dr. Mukwege

"What is life's meaning" asks Dr. Mukwege
"We are here to help others restore their dignity
or our lives make little sense"

Kwanesi is fading from the book of life
a young mother beaten raped left for dead
she cries out hands shaking
"Where is my family have they eaten?"

"Can we help save her?" asks our guest
whose Nobel Prize salutes his fearless devotion
to saving lives near the shores of Lake Kivu
"Good people, why do you stand idly by"
we are humbled by his heart felt words
he makes us feel the depth of Kwanesi's pain
"If one of us is savaged are we all savages?

we sit under the stars at a festive meal
dressed in fine clothes, eating pigeon
careful to avoid the small bones
we dip apples into saucers of honey
wishing everyone a sweet new year
we lift a glass, say "never again"

Dr. Mukwege calls us out
"If evil has no limits it becomes unthinkable
When you ignore the pleas evil takes control
slaughters the innocent in the name of God"

he confronts us with their names
General Coco de Coco and his militia
castrated tortured and killed hundreds
women and children in a single afternoon

The UN High Commission's report goes online
it tells the story in great detail
names the victims not the perpetrators
whose names are locked away forever hidden

No War Today

it was 1936 war was coming
people free only in their secret minds
in Shanghai it was a time
of choosing or being targeted

the stark choice
was to intrigue with the Japanese
or choose between
Nationalists and Communists

passivity becomes the
most dangerous choice
isolation without friends
political rallies looks like state fairs

people in shadows move in stealth
neither known by man
or felt by ghost
only the glitter of the golden era

pleasure permission and
erotic encounters
exotic people parody ancient customs
note on restaurant door: No War Today

The First Battle of Bull Run

boys from North and South
mass in a column by company

as morning drew near whispers of a
great battle send a sudden stir running

like a wave along the lines the momentous
'now' had come wild eyed officers order mayhem

to begin thousands of rifles lowered then aimed to kill
pattering drops then a roll crash roar and rush like mighty

ocean billows upon the shore heavy explosions of the batteries
then the crash of thunderbolts. dead silence as all reload at once.

>>>
>>>

soldiers in blue and grey lay in corn fields watch for shot & shell
shriek and crash canister and bullets whistle high pitch hiss

fiend-like through the air until they could almost see them
every stalk of corn is cut by bullets as if done by a knife

the slain lay in precise rows where they stood in ranks
pile high the death carts that roll across Manassas

their wheels groan under the weight of countless
war dead landscape once lush air perfumed

a mixture corn ragweed clover and blood
drying on beds of crushed corn stalks

turn fields into a monument of death
even a man of god wears a helmet

Defiant Mood in Kharkiv[1]

Ukrainian artillerists the great artists of war set up
a battery to defend their church now standing in ruins.

Brass onion domes are shattered by shrapnel licked by orange flames
their exterior shorn off.

Untouched holy tables shine under large colored pieces of glass.

They slice through penitents caught in the sanctuary as they silently
kneel in prayers for peace.

Russian ordnance lay in all their lazy menace their cylinders
fins & motors crush the Royal Doors.

Guttural sound of rockets resound with drums beats of machine guns
to accompany the bang of artillery.

Roadside billboards show a Kremlin clock tower on a black battleship
swallowed by a Red Sea.

They read "Welcome to Hell you are on our land now soon we will
bury you in it."

[1]Based on "Surviving the Siege of Kharkiv" by James Verini

Ukraine Birthing Clinic[2]

Doc-Lil has served as chief pediatrician
as long as anyone can remember.
Thick set with a determined gait she delivers
babies in an instant with her magic forceps.

The wail of newborns echoes from cribs
and incubators lining hallways while loud
speakers broadcast war bulletins as
classical music plays in the background.

"Mom, comrades are whipping the
Ukrainian men in chains. I'm going crazy
I want to be a good person…that's OK,
that's OK she says, they're not human."

Doc-Lil cuddles Baby Yefimkina a premie
who leads the newborn chorus being
drowned out by a funeral dirge as a coffin
is slowly carried into the cemetery.

"Sergi twists barbed wire into a circle
fashioning an engagement ring.
He drops to one knee and proposes
to Khrystyna, his commanding officer."

Dymid who DocLil delivered is being
buried in silence, as air raid sirens wail
a missile explodes blowing a car
into the birthing clinic's waiting room.

[2]"Barely Started a Life is Ended" by Maria Varenikova; "Voices of War from Russia, Ukraine" by Markus Ziener; "War in Ukraine" by Megan Specia

"Pablo staggers toward the camera
holds out the corpse of a little girl
his once blue eyes now sightless
he asks "is this my darling Lysa""

Doc-Lil rushes back to the NICU,
finds Baby Yefimkina rewraps her pink
 blanket and holds her tight announcing
"I will take care of this baby."

Ghost of War

her eyes
    haunt the night
        she wears
            my dog tags

red slashes
    mark the fallen
        scattered
            in scorched fields

as corpses
    they lay
        on sunflowers
            and carrion

children
    see cuffed hands
        parents
            burned alive

screaming missiles
    wipe towns
        off
            the map

sky
  threatens to fall
        every child
            pushes it up

        some how

James Henry Zukin is an LA based poet active on the Beyond Baroque Foundation Board, Get Lit Advisory Board and co-founder of the Amanda Gorman Future Voices Poetry Prize and Scholarship Contest.

In 1970 he moved to Wall Street as an investment banker. In 1976 he was the co-founder of a small firm in Los Angeles. It was to become a leading global investment bank, Houlihan Lokey. Zukin never stopped writing poetry, even as his work in the financial world grew in scale and scope.

His first book *Poems* was written in calligraphy while at UC Berkeley in the 60's, printed by "La Companie Chelsea" in Montreal. In 2012 he self-published *The Song of Separation* which uses biblical analogies to describe treaties for the division of one country into two states to occur.

Zukin's next work, *Threads*, an 88-page book of poetry drawn from over 1,000 poems written through time with the three threads being introspection, perspective, and expression, was self-published in 2016.

In 2021 he started to enter poetry contests, winning the *Gemini Magazine* Prize for best poem, "Gimp Boy and I," a poignant poem set in a hospital where Covid was raging out of control.

MADCAP was a finalist of the 2022 Finishing Line Press chapbook competition. It is based on experiences as a sovereign debt financial advisor and as an observer of the horrors of war.

Zukin won the 2023 Robert Creeley Prize from Marsh Hawk Press for "Mr. Hand & Ms. Viz," judged by Mary Jo Bang. It stood apart from other works in integrating poetry with economic theory and its evolution over time. Today, his two fields of endeavor have come together and he is a true poet-banker.

www.ingramcontent.com/pod-product-compliance
Lightning Source LLC
Chambersburg PA
CBHW022052080426
42734CB00009B/1316